YAQEEN
STITCHED FROM SORROWS

A Tapestry of ms

Fatima Shaaria Syed, PhD

Copyright © 2024

All rights reserved. No part of this publication may be reproduced, distributed, or transmitted in any form or by any means, including photocopying, recording, or other electronic or mechanical methods, without the prior written permission of the publisher, except in the case of brief quotations embodied in critical reviews and certain other noncommercial uses permitted by copyright law.

ISBN: 978-1-83556-024-2 (Paperback)
ISBN: 978-1-83556-025-9 (eBook)

Cover Design by Aisha Aamir
@incredibleishalllustrations

Book Design by HMDpublishing

Yaqeen (يقين) is an Arabic word generally used to express a state of deep certainty or assurance which means having no doubt about the truth of a matter and arriving at an accurate, doubt-free knowledge

Dedicated to:

*People who are battling with depression,
anxiety and loneliness*

I am, I was, I have been
But what matters the most is
What I am and what I am going to be

Contents

Prologue 15

Part 1.
Despair **21**
Author's Note **23**

The Return 27
Darkness. 28
The Mist 29
Silent Corridors 30
Emptiness 31
Denial 32
Who am I? 33
Lost. 34
The Mask 35
The Regret 36
The Wounded Soul. 37
Loneliness. 38
Anticipation 39
Unshed Tears 40
Trapped. 41
Nothing Lasts. 42
Anxiety - an old friend. 43
Lost Ship. 44
Tears 45
Depression 46

Part 2.
Hope **47**
Author's Note **49**

Acceptance 53
The Scribe 54
The Game of Life 55
Ups and Downs 56
Que Sera Sera 57
Sea of Time 58
Hope 59
Satchel of Memories 60
A Masquerade 61
The Facade 62
A Touch of Insanity 63
True Self 64
Footsteps in the Snow 65
The Song of Silence 66
The Reality 67
Perfect Imperfections 68
Sing Your Own Song 69

Part 3.
Peace **71**
Author's Note **73**

Eternal Peace 77
The Perfect Pearl 78
Metamorphosis 79
The Butterfly 80
The Rise 81
The Relapse 82
I Am 84
This is Me 85
Be Still 86

One Day	87
Life	88
Legacy	90
Alone But Not Lonely	91
Kaleidoscope	92
A Unique Blend	93
The Choice	94
The Ending	95
My Yaqeen	97
About the Author	99

Prologue

Have you ever experienced a moment so profound that it disappeared entirely from your memory? A day that seemed to evaporate into the ether, leaving you waking up with no recollection of where you were, what year it was, or even why you were there? It may sound like a plot for the silver screen but believe me, such inexplicable occurrences do happen in real life.

It happened to me.

I woke up, one fine day, in a hospital bed somewhere in Oxford with a throbbing headache and tubes stuck in me like candles on a birthday cake. I heard beeping, saw faces peering down at me - some strange, some familiar - asking me questions, telling me things. Touching. Probing. Examining. Everything around me was cloaked in a mysteriously dense mist. Shrouded figures, muffled voices, warm hands, and cold needles overpowered by the insistent noise of beeping monitors, excruciating pain and relentless headache. It felt surreal. My mind was a tornado of confusion; tossing questions around like a whirlwind in my head. Where was I? Who were these people? How did I end up here? Only moments ago, I lay sleeping in a dark, silent room, and now, to my astonishment, I found myself thrust into a bewildering world filled with unfamiliar smells, strange sounds, penetrating needles, and overwhelming pain. How did I get here?

It took me a while to realise I was in a hospital. I had an accident. In fact, I was actually waking up from the deep sleep of an induced coma. The year was 2012. The month was February. I was told I was lucky to be alive. I should be grateful for the gift of a second life, but I lay huddled in pain with no appetite for food or people. My battered, sore brain, cocooned in a nest of unwashed, uncombed, and tangled hair, was like a fledgling chirping loudly for some comfort and relief. Confused and hurt, my spirit yearned for solace and care. Those weeks in the hospital were extremely difficult, as I gradually pieced together the reasons for my shattered body, traumatized brain, fragmented memories, and disrupted life.

Encircled by well-wishers, their caring hearts determined to mend both my body and soul, I faced a haunting void in my memory which was imploring me to uncover the truth of that ill-fated January night. Questions and more questions roared within me like a tempest on a mad stampede: How did the accident happen? Why did the oncoming car evade my sight? What caused me to suddenly swerve in front of it? Did I not hear or see it approaching? And as my car dangled precariously over the bridge, what were my thoughts and my feelings? Could I hear the desperate sirens of the fire engines, the police cars and the ambulance? The relentless banging on my window. The shouts of concerns for my well-being. The tug of the fire engines as they pulled me back to safety. Was I scared? Did I pray? Was I aware that my life hung in the balance?

It was a mild, dry January night when the car accident happened and I woke up to a wet, snowy February afternoon. Six days had passed before I became aware of my surroundings. Unknowingly and unintentionally, I had lost precious days of my life. Yet, I lay in my hospital bed oblivious to what I had lost and what awaited me.

People often say: 'be careful what you wish for'. Ironically, I had received exactly what I had prayed for, but in the most unexpected manner. Prior to the accident, I remember waking up each morning, even after a restful night, yearning for more sleep. Looking back, the reason for my weariness was clear: managing the school and social schedules of two teenagers as a single mom while working full-time was utterly draining and exhausting. Thus, waking up from a coma, though bewildering, felt like a twisted answer to my silent pleas for prolonged rest and sleep.

Time and again, I had to disappoint my family, my friends, and the police as I kept repeating, "I don't remember." The moments leading up to the accident, the drive itself, and the harrowing crash were still locked away in obscurity. That ill-fated January day, when it all transpired, remained shrouded under the cloak of amnesia. Even now, memories of that fateful night continue to elude me. Yet intriguingly, I hold onto shards of memory from the time I was unconscious. I remember being surrounded by sleeping bodies in a room that was murky, dark, and sombre, yet surprisingly tranquil. It was as though I was in the Sleeping Beauty castle, where life simply stood still. Another memory is when I heard someone near me gasping for air. They sounded as if they were in excruciating pain and deep distress. I remember praying for them - asking God to ease their pain. Little did I realize that I might have been hearing my own struggle with breathing and praying for myself.

One more moment, now eternally etched in my memory is when I tried to pull the plastic tube from my nose, believing it to be the cause of my ragged breathing. My attempts were in vain as both my hands were tightly bound with white gauze bandages, as if I was wearing boxing gloves. In my desperation, I remember begging profusely with the nurse to set my hands free. I am not sure if she could hear my cries, but I remember slipping back into unconsciousness, still pleading. Looking back, the irony of that moment is not lost on me: the tube I was so eager to remove was the very thing keeping me alive.

After a difficult few weeks in the hospital, I came home to heal. As time passed on, days morphed into weeks and weeks into months. The void in my memory slowly began to fill with versions of the event narrated by others. I can now recount with clarity what happened, when it occurred, and how it unfolded, but it is neither my story nor my experience. Like a gifted seamstress, I have interwoven the accounts of others to blanket the one glaring truth – I still do not remember.

Yet, amidst the fragments of lost recollections, one thing remains vividly clear: the path of healing and recovery I had inadvertently embarked on. The journey of recovery was arduous and fraught with long gruelling moments of bleakness but occasionally, within those dark shadows, flickers of hope and joy would emerge. I endured the ebbs and flow of loss and pain, navigated through the storms of mood swings and depression, and faced endless battles with pain and pills. The conflict within me was profound - a continuous tug-of-war between gratitude for the gift of life and a longing for the blissful oblivion of eternal sleep.

Each day, I fought to rise above the weight of other people's expectations and my own, the financial burden of unemployment, the legal strife to retain my driving license, and the ongoing emotional turmoil within that threatened my sanity. However, guided by an invisible force, I found myself navigating slowly and rather ineptly through this dark sea of despair. My quest of healing led me to people, places, and activities that helped me make sense of my inner chaos. While the physical wounds have mended over time, the emotional scars persist. Even now, I battle with my inner demons. Most days I win but some days I simply give in.

This collection of poems was born out of my struggle to find joy and purpose in being alive after a close encounter with death. Each verse encapsulates my quest to emerge from the depths of depression and loneliness to discover peace and harmony in the simple act of being alive. The words in this book flowed from my soul during moments of deep anguish and pain. Therefore, I would never class myself as a 'poet' but as a custodian of words which were born out of the throes of an emotional inferno within to help me heal and thrive.

Within these verses I, unknowingly, chronicled a journey from self-loathing to self-belief and self-love. These poems encapsulate my struggles with depression, loneliness, anxiety, and both physical and emotional pain. As I grew stronger – physically, mentally, emotionally, and spiritually – my poems evolved too. Darkness giving way to light.

This book brings together poems written over a decade from 2012 to 2022, and is divided into three sections that reflect the different stages of my recovery: Despair, Hope, and Peace.

Section 1: Despair

These poems capture the darkest moments when I was in deep depression and the will to live had all but vanished. Overwhelmed physically and mentally, I wrestled with loneliness, anxiety, fatigue and pain. All the while striving to make sense of my shattered reality.

Section 2: Hope

As I came to terms with my situation, I began seeking help to navigate through the emotional abyss I had found myself in. The poems in this section reflect the nascent flicker of hope that emerged as I started embracing my circumstances. Gradually, realisation turned into acceptance and acceptance into hope.

Section 3: Peace

The poems in this final section bear witness to my journey of reconciliation with myself and my experiences. As I achieved a growing sense of self-awareness and self-worth, I set forth on a path of self-love and self-belief.

I share these poems hoping they might resonate with some of you by offering the same consolation that they have provided me. May you discover within these verses, a token of wisdom to aid you on your journey of healing. May you find inspiration to seek solace, hope, and purpose on your own unique path through life. May my words inspire you to persevere and continually believe in your own strength.

My message is one of hope, faith, and trust. Beyond the darkness, there is always a guiding light. Our journey requires only that we press on, fortified by an unwavering belief in ourselves - Yaqeen.

These words spoke to me.
I hope they might speak to you too.

PART 1
Despair

Author's Note

Depression is a ghastly place to be in. Yet, paradoxically, it also clasps you in a warm embrace, creating a cocoon that seemingly shields you from the outside world. The illusory sense of safety beckons even more enticingly, tempting you to plunge deeper into its inviting abyss. Its allure is so comforting that you are tempted to stay enclosed in its deceptive comfort and let the world drift by. Depression is neither an easy state to be in nor an easy state to leave. The battle is real, and the journey to recovery is gruelling. But having emerged on the other side, I can attest to the importance of clinging to any glimmer of hope that surfaces amidst the engulfing darkness of helplessness and hopelessness.

Following the accident, I grappled with significant losses - financial, emotional, and physical. I was made redundant while embroiled in a year-long legal battle, defending myself against charges of 'dangerous driving.' Despite being the victim of a high-speed collision and sustaining severe injuries, I was confronted with the possibility of receiving a three-year criminal record and a jail sentence, putting my eligibility for British citizenship at risk. Moreover, my ability to seek new employment was hampered by struggles with temporary memory loss, extreme fatigue, constant headaches, and sensitivity to light and noise. During that time, my physical and mental strength waned. But most profoundly, there was a deep erosion of my connection to the very essence of being alive, accompanied by a disheartening detachment from the joy and purpose of living. In fact, I lost my invincible belief and faith in life itself and what it had to offer - my Yaqeen.

I was caught in a maelstrom of physical, emotional, and financial distress. I found myself drowning in self-pity and regret. So fixated on what I had lost that I became oblivious to the abundant love and support extended by my family and friends. During this turbulent period of my life, I found myself grappling with the weight of judgment and societal expectations. People say surviving a life-altering accident usually evokes a profound sense of gratitude and a new sense of purpose but I felt nothing except self-pity and pain. While I valued the second chance at life, the burden of aligning with people's expectations of how I should feel and behave was immense. I was confused and unable to understand why I was not undergoing the expected inner and spiritual transformation typically associated with a near-death experience.

Contrary to feeling relief, joy, and elation, I found myself distanced from such sentiments. The accident did not bring me any closer to God, nor did it bestow upon me a renewed sense of purpose. Instead, I felt the opposite – an overwhelming sense of misfortune and bad luck as everything seemed to be collapsing around me. The persistent thought that 'living was onerous and dying was effortless' played like a broken record in my mind haunting me day and night.

Trying to grasp the essence of gratitude in the midst of such upheaval proved to be a formidable task. This was not the first time that life had thrown unexpected challenges upon me. In my twenties, widowhood thrust upon me the role of a sole carer and provider for my two young children. My life's path shifted dramatically, propelling me into the unfamiliar role of a single parent. I left my homeland in search of a new beginning in the West for both my children and myself. But just as I was putting down roots in my new country, fate once again intervened and shook the very foundations of my existence.

The poems in these sections were written when I was in a state of extreme depression made worse by the persistent pain and fatigue. I was stuck in a cycle of massive mood swings – one moment feeling I am in control and the very next feeling helpless, lonely, and misunderstood. Things, circumstances and people seemed stacked against me. I was fighting to keep hold of my senses, my driving license, my job and my nationality while plagued by temporary memory loss, extreme sensory sensitivity, continuous headaches, muscle pain, and insomnia. If those were not enough things to deal with, I also felt I had to manage people's expectations which at that time felt unrealistic and burdensome. All I wanted was to disappear and never re-surface. Life was hard but letting go of the deceptive security and comfort of depression was even harder.

Unbeknownst to me, I had hit rock bottom.

I lost faith. I lost hope. I lost myself. I was stuck in a raging torrent of emotions. On numerous occasions, I felt compelled to surrender and escape from this relentlessly demanding life to find peace on the other side. It was the darkest chapter of my life when I lay confined to my bed questioning the very essence of my existence. During those moments, death appeared almost like a kindred spirit.

Over this period, things took a turn for the worse. I sank deeper into self-pity, feeling more isolated and lonelier than ever before. Swallowed by agony and despair, I found myself completely at a loss and uncertain about what lay ahead. While everyone around me expected me to keep going, all I longed for was to close my eyes and surrender.

I felt as if I was in a pressure cooker
The pressure was intensifying
And, I was crumbling

The Return

I look death in the eye and death stared back
Silently, quietly, patiently
Waiting, anticipating, biding
Ready to grasp me when my time comes.
I touched briefly
The darkness, the stillness, the quietness
And oh, the sweet warmth of its embrace
Alas, like a cruel mistress
Death spurns me
Coldly, sharply, deliberately
Back to where I came from
Leaving me wanting more.
Life beckons me
Enticing me, inviting me, tempting me
A butterfly emerging from its chrysalis
Tentatively, cautiously, hesitantly
Life coaxes me out
Readily wraps me, cuddles me, hugs me
In a warm embrace.
Life endearingly holds onto me
While death waits patiently in the wings.

~ ❖ ~

Darkness

Darkness stalks me
Watching quietly
Waiting patiently
For me to slip
Like a hungry hound
Straining at its leash
Smelling the scent of misery
Ready to jump
And, shred to pieces
My very being.
To my tired soul
The desire to cut loose
Is like a siren's song
Luring me to my end
My wilting soul
Slowly succumbing
Gently surrending.
Light is cold
Darkness - warm
And, welcoming.

~ ❖ ~

The Mist

Yet again, my heart bleeds
For I am alone
Lonelier than ever before
Lost in the cold, dark, eternal emptiness
The barren forsaken void haunting me
Eerily silent and forlorn
Watching and waiting
Is this how life is supposed to be
An ongoing untouchable relationship
Is there reality somewhere
Is there substance somewhere
Is there trust, belief, and certainty somewhere
I touch gold and it turns into dust
Dust that swirls around my feet
Wrapping me, yet again
In the mist of uncertainty.

~ ❖ ~

Silent Corridors

Me and my weary soul trudge
The empty corridors of life
Vastness as colossal as the space
Emptiness as deep as the ocean
Quietness as still as death
Yet we plod on
Weary and incomplete
Momentarily, the ring of a child's laughter
A giggle, a playful poke
A tease, a mischief, a joke
Creates excitement, and
Hope!
Breaking the stillness
The dullness
The purposelessness.
Re-energised and reactivated
The soul rejoices
But, only temporarily
As it is engulfed
Yet again,
By the vast empty silence within.
Reality reigns
Slowly, but steadily
Darkness takes over.

~ ❖ ~

Emptiness

Do you want to see what emptiness looks like?
Peer into my eyes
Do you want to see what emptiness sounds like?
Listen to my heart
Do you want to know what emptiness feels like?
Caress my tears
There's hurt
There's pain
There's complete stillness
Nothing moves except darting pain
A sense of deep loss
Of broken trust
Of loneliness
Standing forlornly amid
The dark dense sea of life
What love
What relationships
All slave to personal gain
Do you want to know what emptiness is?
Watch me
A shell of a person
Slowly crumbling
Under the weight of love and expectations
A shadow of who I was
And, who I could have been.

~ ❖ ~

Denial

In stillness, I lie
Amidst the encompassing cold darkness
Pierced only by the glow of a small lamp
I wonder:
Is the coldness outside or inside me?
Is the stillness outside or inside me?
Is the darkness outside or inside me?
My smile hides many of my scars
My laugh masks my bleeding heart
My twinkling eyes deny the ache inside
As I lay wondering
Who am I fooling
The world
Or
Simply myself.

~ ❖ ~

Who am I?

Who am I, truly, and what lies within
Behind my smile, hidden scars reside
My laughter cloaks the inner din
Bright eyes belie the ache inside
Who am I
And, what will I be
This thought vanishes with a sigh
What's left behind is a shell of me.

~❖~

Lost

I am lost somewhere between
The past and the future
Friendship and love
Loyalty and betrayal
Things that have been said and done
And the things that are going to be said and done.
I am lost somewhere between
The now and then
The then and now
The end and the beginning
Frozen in the present
Weighed down by the past
Frightened stiff by the future
I look around bewildered
Astray in the storm of time.
I am lost somewhere between
Believe and disbelieve
Trust and distrust
Leaving and staying
Haunted by memories
Scared of losing
Petrified of rejection
Adrift in the milieu of words
Playing havoc with my mind
Where a lot is said but nothing done
Nothing said but a lot is done.
I am lost somewhere
Between here and there
Now and then.

~❖~

The Mask

Sometimes we laugh, so as not to weep
Smile, so as not to cry
Masking what we feel deep inside
A cold wintry sun hiding the dark clouds
Of pain, sorrow and despair
Smile, a beacon in the storm of tears
Laughter, a storm to drown the tears
Happiness, sadness
Love, hate
Joy, sorrow
An intermittent play of shadow and light.
Sadness to mask the warmth of happiness
Happiness to eliminate the coldness of sorrow
A game of emotions we play
Laughter with a ring of sorrow
A smile with a halo of pain
The unending dance
Of pleasure and pain.

~ ❖ ~

The Regret

The endless hours of
Squabbling
Shouting
Screaming
The tears of frustration
The fury
The tempest
The lashing out
Mouth as volatile as lava spewing volcano
Words as hard as cold firm granite
Eyes as dry as sun-baked desert
Heart as cold as a block of ice
Hands shaking like quivering leaves amid a storm
Mind hot and red as burning coals
Emotions on extra adrenaline
Fury, a ferocious tornado
Destroying everything in its path
Broken, spent and exhausted
Claimed slowly by the descending calm
The stillness
The quietness
The awareness
Signalling the end of complete madness
Setting in of remorse
Of losing control
Of hurting
Of temporary insanity
The many faces of irreversible regret.

~✦~

The Wounded Soul

I feel your deep hidden pain, old friend
The hurt that's become a cloak
The smile that's become your mask
The false lilt in your voice
The silent empty laughter
Erupting from the hollow chambers of your soul.
You bleed silently, dear friend
Whilst I watch you, helplessly
Fall apart
Fragment by fragment
Piece by piece.
I am but a quiet, mournful spectator
Of the drama of life
Unfolding gradually
Bit by bit
Piece by piece
Moment by moment.
All the while, wanting to scream
Stop! dear friend
I am here for you!
I do understand!
I do care!
Yet, no sound escapes
To halt the splintering of, yet
Another fragment of my wounded soul
Falling mercilessly but silently
Around my bleeding self.

~ ❖ ~

Loneliness

Loneliness gnaws at me relentlessly
Biting constantly at my inner peace
Wearing away my inner contentment
My smile hiding years of pain
My laugh shadowing an eternity of inner conflict
I am strong yet, fragile
Delicate as a blooming rose
Crumbling with the slightest whiff
Of love and words of comfort
Bruised and battered from inside
Wanting love and comfort
Yet, remain enclosed in loneliness
Wanting to be left alone
Don't pity me!
Don't feel sorry for me!
Don't come to me in remorse!
Come only if you really care for me
If not, then just leave me alone.

~ ❖ ~

Anticipation

With a heavy heart
And a broken soul
Trembling under the weight of memories
Running amok with emotions
The darkness rises from deep within
Rushing upwards for release
Engulfing my very being
Darkness overcoming the light
Coldness overpowering the warmth
Hardness overshadowing the softness.
As intense pain pierces the heart
The soul screams in protest
Tears rush up to the eyes
Waiting tentatively for release.
The world stops for a while
A moment stretched into eternity
A drop of water
Frozen, on the tip of a waterfall
Waiting, hoping, wanting, longing
For a quick escape.

~ ❖ ~

Unshed Tears

The stage is set
Time stands still
Like a hissing volcano ready to erupt
An earthen dam cracking under the assault
Nerves taut, eyes full
Brimming with unshed tears
Yearning to wash away the pain
Yet, not a drop rolls
You have cried so much
That even the tears refuse to fall.

~ ❖ ~

Trapped

I want to run away but where will I run to?
I want to hide but where will I hide?
There's no escape
There's no end
You just have to keep on playing
This game of ups and downs
One breath in and one out
One foot up and one down
One step forward, two steps back
The journey continues
Slithering through the snaky paths
Of unfulfilled dreams and desires.
Though paths keep changing
The destination remains the same.
Your heart might be bruised
Your feet sore
Your body aching
Your soul in pain
Exhausted from the turbulent journey
Of emotions galore.
Losses, gains, happiness and sadness
Love, hate, friendship and enmity
Births, deaths, laughter and, tears
All takes its toll.
Yet, the journey continues mercilessly
Under the bleeding feet of the pilgrim soul.

~ ❖ ~

Nothing Lasts

Nothing lasts forever, or does it
Memories whispers in my ears
Of the joys of days gone by
The sights, the smells, the sounds
Of places and people that once held me
Enthralled in their embrace
The old dusty corridors of my childhood
Beckons me with open arms
To walk me down memory lane
I see myself lying in front of a fireplace
On a cold January day
The smell of freshly made pakoras
Playing havoc with my senses
I hear giggles erupting in laughter
Rippling with innocent dreams
I feel love wrapping me
Securely in a tight clasp
Enticing me to lay my head down
For always, in peace.
Nothing lasts forever, or does it
Tightly bound and hidden
In the secret passages of our mind.

~❖~

Anxiety - an old friend

I saw a child
Frightened and confused
Face white as snow
Eyes red as blood
Mind grey as mist
Sweaty and trembling
Peering into emptiness
Jumping at every sound
Flustered and perturbed
Wide-eyed and scared
Dried mouth and sweaty palmed
Heart throbbing widly
Trembling ever so slightly
Screaming it's too much
Overload! sensory overload!
Give me time, give me space
Wriggling inside an invisible cage
Like crumpled paper bobbing
In the strong wind.
Run! Run! Run!
Eyes shout while the heart gallops
Heedless and wild
Ten thousand black horses gone astray
Who is this?
This shaken, pitiful, lost creature
Staring back at me with those wilful eyes
Go away! Go away!
Yet nothing moves.
In that moment of stillness
I see myself
Staring back at me.

~ ❖ ~

Lost Ship

I feel I'm drowning
Being sucked vigorously into a vortex
Of despair and self-pity
Surrounded by a whirlpool of
Unfulfilled desires and unmet expectations
Insistent thoughts
If only things could be different.
I am struggling
To stay afloat the monstrous waves of
Unfulfilled wishes, and dreams
Bashing me relentlessly against
The rocks of fate and bitter reality.
In these choppy waters of time
Desperately seeking a straw of hope
To keep me afloat
A simple beacon of light
To pull me out
Before I disappear into complete oblivion
Lost forever, in the storms of life
Torn, battered, beaten
Not knowing where I'm heading.
The seas of life will calm eventually
The straw of hope will be found ultimately
The ray of light will shine finally
But where will I be then
What will have become of me
A lost ship might find its way
But, is it where it wants to be.

~ ❖ ~

Tears

When all has been said and done
There's nothing left to apologise for
There's nothing left to forgive
The erupting emotions
Die down
Lying dormant
Covered in the ashes of spoken words
And, potent unshed tears
Amidst the smouldering debris
Of relationships lost
Trust broken; egos smashed
Wells up a single tear
Rolling down slowly
Through the landscape of sadness
Regret, loneliness, and emptiness
Leaving a desolate trail
There's nothing left
To say, do or pray
But to simply surrender
To yourself
To your life
To your reality
Tears are what you had
Tears are what you have
And tears are what you'll have
For now, and always.

~❖~

Depression

To be depressed
Or not to be depressed
Is not a choice
But a state of being
Entering it
Just happens
Leaving it
A choice…

~ ❖ ~

PART 2
Hope

Author's Note

When you hit rock bottom, you have two choices: either to drown or to rise.

It was in February 2013, a year after my accident, that I was at my most vulnerable. Days blurred as I alternated between crying, sleeping, and crying some more. I had never felt so lonely, so lost, and so helpless. In a span of a year, I had lost everything - my job, my health, my memory, and my right to British citizenship - all due to circumstances beyond my control. A car accident happened and life as I knew it was over.

This section of poems reflect my constant struggle to come to terms with my present. I found memories of the past clashing with my own expectations. Depression is a strange place to be in where even the most well-meaning comments seem false and accusing. You feel insecure and unwanted as if caught up in a charade. The thoughts that 'the world would be better off without me' crossed my mind several times. For months I remained in this trance of hurt, helplessness and hopelessness. Yet, there was something indefinable inside me that refused to let me give up on myself and on life itself. Even through the bleakest of days, this indomitable spirit yearned to live, breathe and to endure.

Hope emerged. Slowly but surely, life started dragging me back to itself.

I remember vividly the day when a glimmer of hope pierced through my despair. Lying in bed, consumed by hunger and exhaustion from endless crying, my young children approached to comfort me. In the warmth of their embrace, a powerful realization crystallized: 'My children need and depend on me.'

It served as a reminder that I had a responsibility to set things right for them, and therefore, 'surrender' was not an option. Even though my meticulously planned world had fallen apart once again, all was not lost. Whether I accepted it or not, I was alive. Despite the towering challenges, I knew I had to forge ahead for my children. The gnawing pangs of hunger were a jarring reminder that, while my soul might crave release, my body clung to life tenaciously. From this profound awakening, an unshakeable conviction emerged, rising like a phoenix from the ashes: For the sake of my children, " I wanted not only to live but to thrive!"

This epiphany became my purpose - my ikigai.

With this realization, acceptance began to take root. A small flicker of hope transformed into a blazing fire. I came to terms with the fact that the events that happened to me were beyond my control. I could not have prevented the car from hitting me. The loss of my job was unavoidable. Declaring "not guilty" would not have guaranteed a win in court. Most importantly, I realized I could not turn back time to retrieve my job, my memory, or the life I once knew. However, I could embrace the present. I accepted the gaps in my memory, my diminished energy, fluctuating moods, persistent pain, sleepless nights, bouts of depression and fatigue and most importantly, my new reality. I chose to acknowledge the person I had become, rather than yearn for who I once was. Slowly, my "cant's" evolved into "wills".

I consistently reminded myself that while I might not remember now, there would come a day when memories will return. Despite feeling drained both emotionally and physically, I held onto the belief that I would fully recover, eventually. I learned to pace myself and adjust my expectations. I mastered driving without succumbing to panic attacks every time I pulled out of the driveway. I learnt to manage pain and function without sedatives and antidepressants. I acquired techniques to navigate the roller coaster of emotions and the debilitating grip of fatigue and anxiety. To manage my temporary memory loss, I began carrying a notebook, diligently jotting down notes and formulating questions before consultations with my doctor or other service providers. From using a notebook, I transitioned to recording my questions, thoughts, and even my poems on my mobile phone. Consequently, the 'notes' feature on my mobile phone has evolved into a trusted ally.

Instead of constantly comparing my current state to the past, I started measuring my progress from one week to the next. By accepting who I had become and taking each day as it came, I started noticing the subtle improvement in both my physical and mental strength. When I embraced my circumstances, belief in myself and the world around me started to flourish. I understood and grasped this universal truth: *while I can not always control life's events, the power to shape my response lies firmly in my hands.* This profound realisation fundamentally changed my perspective on what happened to me and became the compass that steered me towards recovery and reignited my will to live. I finally glimpsed the ray of light I had been desperately seeking. Without realising it, I had embarked on a journey towards self-love and self-worth.

Acceptance, courage, self-awareness, and determination served as my lifelines, drawing me out of the profound abyss of despair I had, unintentionally, descended into. When I gradually let them in, the love and care of my friends and family anchored me during my struggle with depression. While their support reignited my determination to push forward, the feelings of loneliness and dejection frequently enticed me to give up on myself. Despite the pull of depression, the promise I had made to myself and my children, continually motivated me to heal and recover.

Slowly and steadily, I began to rebuild myself with faith and the power of certainty - Yaqeen.

With realisation comes acceptance
And, with acceptance comes healing

Acceptance

The picture of you is fading
Like a pencil sketch being erased
Tenderly by the hands of time
Not a day go by
When an overwhelming desire to see you
Surges over me like a rising wave
You were but just a writing
On the sands of time
Washed away for ever
Yet, your footsteps remain
Eternally imprinted on my soul
There's acceptance
There's peace
There's courage
Wrapped in the halo of hope
Whilst I wait patiently
To carve, yet another story
On the dunes of my life
Only, for it to be erased
Once again
By the gusts of time.

~❖~

The Scribe

The pen of life is continuously inscribing our stories
Weaving a web of histories
Dipping in and out of the ink of destiny
Brushing a touch of fate in all its entity
A kaleidoscope of past, present, and future
To remember, to relish, to savour, and nurture
Who knows
When the ink runs out
Or, the pen breaks.
With each stroke a new twist, a new turn
A moment lost or an entirety earned
Life keeps scribbling
A romance, a tragedy, a comedy, or a gripping drama
Leaving it to us to create
An epic, a fable, a legend or a saga
The writer writes the story
The actor plays the part
Till the curtain falls
And
You depart.

~ ❖ ~

The Game of Life

I don't need your pity nor your admiration
I simply need your acceptance
I would be adored!
And, you would've been abandoned
I would be comfortable!
And, you would've been struggling
I would be cherished!
And, you would've been forsaken
Life is but just a game of cards
It's the hand that you are dealt with
All aces or all jacks
All kings or all jokers
A throw of dice
A show of hands
A turn of the wheel
And your fate is sealed
Winners become losers
Losers become winners
Such is the game of life
Play it hard
Play it well
Play it fair.

~ ❖ ~

Ups and Downs

Life is pretty strange
But, at times stranger
If it was meant to be
It will happen
What happened was meant to be
A surging wave has to crash
A soaring star has to plummet
A rising sun has to set
And, a healing heart
Has to break
Till there's nothing left
To say, feel or regret.

~ ❖ ~

Que Sera Sera

Calm resides where there was a storm
Acceptance presides where there was denial
Peace abides where there was a frenzy
A hush dwells where there was turbulence
Engulfing, overwhelming, all consuming
Tranquillity, apathy, and indifference
Whatever will be, will be.

~ ❖ ~

Sea of Time

Let your past be like
Footsteps in the sand
Washed away by the waves of time
What is done is done
And, cannot be undone
Let your past sleep like
A princess in the fairy tale
Woken only by the kiss of a happy time
The could haves and the should haves
Are simply regrets keeping you awake.
Let your past go with gentleness,
Like, a feather floating softly
Through the expanse of time
Never say never
As there is always a next time
Mistakes are to be made
Lessons are to be learnt
Memories are to be created
So, let your past drown
Tenderly, in the sea of time.

~❖~

Hope

The faint echoes of the past
Sometime reverberates relentlessly
Transporting me to a place
Lost long ago
Resounding with the murmurs
Of who I once was
A princess of my father's castle
Cocooned in my safe world
The ghost of times gone by
Haunts me relentlessly
With bittersweet memories
Whispers of laughter
Overshadowed by cries of loss
Radiance of love
Overpowered by the gloom of betrayal
Tenderness of care
Overwhelmed by the coldness of neglect
Warmth of attention
Overcome by the harshness of loneliness
In the darkness of the silent night
Memories descend quietly
Humming sweet nothingness
Rustling up dormant feelings.
There is no regret
There is no guilt
There is no heartache
As a little voice inside
Assures me persistently, that
All is not lost
I was cherished once
And, I would be cherished again.

~ ❖ ~

Satchel of Memories

As I travel through the wilderness of life
Collecting moments in my satchel of memories
Leaving a trail of breadcrumbs
To help me find my way back
I capture events
Hoarding them
Where only, I can touch
Every smile, every touch, every word
Enshrined in time
As if touched by Midas
Brightly lighting my path
From present to the future.
In my times of loneliness
And, profound sadness
I delve deep into my chest of memories
Drawing out happy moments
Like a cluster of pearls
Complete when bound together
I roll each moment lovingly
Twisting and turning gently
The rosary of my life.
Somewhere inside me
A voice whispers gently
It's only when the petals split
That a flower blooms
And it's only in a moment's bosom
That a memory is born.

~ ❖ ~

A Masquerade

Life is a game
A play
A drama
A charade
You are in
As long as
You can keep to the script
Hold on tightly to your mask
And, play the upbeat character
The world wants you to be
A mere slip
A glimpse
A peek
Of your inner turmoil
Make the curtains come down
Defences go up
People move on
And, you are left on your own
Hypocrisy is what makes the world go around
Pretend and you will be loved
Lie and you will be believed
Laugh and you will be joined
Cry and you will be abandoned
So, don the mask
Put on the fake smile
Play by the rules
After all, life is
Just a facade
Merely, a masquerade.

~❖~

The Facade

Where's truth?
Where's sincerity?
Where's real self?
Under the layers of social dust
Amassed over the years
It is hard to find authenticity
The mask fused with the core
All fake, fabricated and false
The twinkling eyes belying the wrath inside
The beaming smile hiding the inner bitterness
The friendly gestures covering deep resentment
Leaving you wondering
Who to trust
And, who not to.

~ ❖ ~

A Touch of Insanity

There's a little madness in each one of us
A grain of insanity
There's wickedness in purity
Happiness in tears
A smudge in what is pristine
A shine in something dull
A ray of hope in despair
Shadow in sunshine
And, death with life.
Every cloud has its silver lining
Every dog has its day
What rises must fall
What falls must rise
What is started must end
What has ended must start
There are no ends but only beginnings
A birth, a rebirth, and a birth again
For within our touch of insanity
Life truly ensues
Just as an oyster's tears create a pearl
A cocoon's silky threads bear a butterfly
Life's trials shape us
To make us who we are.

~ ❖ ~

True Self

I walk through the valley of life
Overshadowed by towering egos
Surrounded by fake pride
Overcast by bulging ambitions
Finding true friends
A quest in itself
In this masquerade of life
Everyone has donned masks
Pretentious, pompous or pious
The exterior negating the interior
As one mask slips, it is
Quickly replaced by another.
People meet; people leave
The masquerade continues
Faces remain unchanged
Cold, hard and lifeless
Dancing to the beat of the
Ever evolving greedy world
And I
Keep searching for my true self.

~ ❖ ~

Footsteps in the Snow

The places you have touched
The people you have met
The uncertainties, the anguish, the doubts
The questions that remain unanswered
The pain, the loss, the hurt
Throbbing in every fibre of your being
A constant reminder of who you were
And what could have been.
Yet, what was, is no longer there
And what will, is yet to come
Like footsteps in the snow
One day they are there
The next no more.
To recreate one has to wait
For the first winter snow
Yet, it's never the same
Neither the steps nor the snow
Each step, a new journey
Each journey, a new destination
Taking you where you have never been
And, where you will never ever go again
It's not where you are that matters
Or where you have been
But, where you are going.

~ ❖ ~

The Song of Silence

I hear music in the emptiness of unspoken words
Shadows dancing to the tune of hanging words
Heartbroken but enraptured by love
Even in silence, there is a roar
Of unmet dreams
Of unexpressed desire
Of unvoiced pain.
Only the feet of the unfulfilled
Tap to the melody of the silent symphony
In the empty chambers of the heart
Dancing on broken promises
Swinging on vines of rejection
A litany of love
Bouncing off the pulpit of denial.
Only in the quiet stillness
The drumrolls of hope can be heard
Reaching a crescendo
In the pulsating stillness
Vibrant and alive
Intoxicated with hope
Swirling, swaying, spinning
Higher and higher!
Shattering the silence
Of the Silent.

~ ❖ ~

The Reality

We yearn
For the past
For the love of people long gone
For the times yet to unfold
For the things out of our reach
Craving attention, recognition
Or just plain simple, obscurity.
We wait
To be transported to pastures anew
To things to transpire
To find delight in the caverns of our fantasy
To frolic whimsically
Amongst mountains and valleys of our imagination
Or just hide in the deepest recess of our thoughts
Fabricating sandcastles of
Wishes, dreams, and desires
Only for them to be swept away
With a single stroke of destiny
In fact, with a simple brush with reality.
Nevertheless, dream on
And, let your spirit soar high
For in the dance between dreams and reality
Lies the true magic of stories yet to unfold.

~❖~

Perfect Imperfections

Just when the sun reaches its zenith
The earth pulls away
Just as the rose blooms to glory
The petal drifts apart
Just as the path starts straightening
The junction splits the road
Each ending, a return to a new beginning
Each beginning, a start to a new ending.
How far are you able to sail
If the wind didn't help.
How exciting can be your journey
If there were no bends on the way
How deep can your love be
If it can't withstand separation
For every fall, there's a rise
For every tear, there's a smile
For every loss, there's a win.
Perfection never makes life complete
Imperfection is what makes life perfect
Our perfect Imperfections.

~ ❖ ~

Sing Your Own Song

You are the author of your own story
The central character in all its glory
Create a tale worth remembering
Not a composition worth dismissing
You are your own song
Sing it out resoundingly
Till the time you 're gone.

~❖~

PART 3
Peace

Author's Note

Emerging from one of life's harshest trials, I found a revitalised sense of self. Every new day became a testament to resilience and hope. What were once laborious acts – like getting out of bed, brushing my teeth, or slipping into a fresh pair of clothes – became daily affirmations of my continued existence. My pale anxious reflection in the mirror evolved into a symbol of fortitude.

My healing journey led to not just external transformations but also to a profound internal metamorphosis. Recognizing that my circumstances were beyond control, I found myself compelled to embark on the daunting task of self-transformation. This path was about defying the constraints of my situation, and choosing to work hard on myself to become the embodiment of my aspirations. My healing demanded more than just finding light amidst the darkness; it challenged me to become the very essence of light.

This collection of poems traces my turbulent path towards self-realization, acceptance, and healing, punctuated by moments of self-doubt, uncertainty, and loneliness.

Life seldom charts a straight path. Much like a river, it meanders and twists bringing with it a mix of unpredictable challenges and quite often concealed blessings. At times, despair threatened to engulf me. Yet, much like peeling the layers of an onion, with each challenge faced and surmounted, I delved deeper into my inner self, gradually revealing more of my true essence..

There are still days when I feel sad, lost, and lonely; when the burdens of existence appear to want to drag me back into the old quagmire of despair and self-pity. The unmistakable signs manifest. Tears brim, and a tide of sorrow sweeps in like descending mists on a cold December evening, murmuring suggestions to surrender to my weariness and never rise again. Various voices chime in, questioning my will and purpose. "Give up," one voice whispers. "You are not needed," another echoes. "Poor you! You must be so tired of fighting this relentless battle of existence," a third chimes in. "Why do you even want to live?" another voice demands. Amidst this cacophony of doubting voices, a tiny but resolute voice within me asserts its defiance: 'I want to live for my children, for myself, and for the sheer gift of life itself!' I anchor myself to this resilient, unwavering inner voice and the discouraging whispers gradually fade away.

Many challenges persist, with ghosts from the past occasionally casting their shadow over the present. To this day, hearing sirens and seeing rushing ambulances causes my heart to sink a little and the hair on the back of neck rise with fear. Although I do not remember my journey in the ambulance to the hospital, my body somehow does at a deeper level. This makes me realise that even when we think we have overcome adversities and healed, remnants of our old self remain hidden within us.

Life's rich tapestry of experiences, from ecstatic joys to crushing lows, has painted my soul in brilliant hues. Having journeyed through depression and loneliness, I see myself as a traveller through life experienced in navigating the extensive terrain of emotions. Emotions, whether turbulent or serene, have become my constant companions teaching me the depth and breadth of not only my very own being but also of human existence. There were times when I found myself teetering on the brink of depression, where 'giving in' felt like the easier and simpler option. Yet, as time passed, I discerned the value and teachings hidden even within the bleakest moments. Now, rather than stifling my all consuming and intense emotions, I wholeheartedly embrace them and listen to what they are trying to tell me.

I have learned that everything in life is transient, including life itself. Nothing lasts forever – neither the sorrowful times nor the joyous ones. Everything must end. The impermanence of both sorrow and joy is an inescapable truth of life - a promise that accompanies us from our very first breath. With this in mind, I consciously strive each day to cultivate gratitude, directing my attention towards the present: 'what is' rather than lingering on 'what might have been.'

During this period, I drew inspiration from renowned thought leaders such as Viktor Frankl, who revealed the human capacity to find meaning in suffering; Maya Angelou, emphasizing resilience and self-empowerment through her poetry; Dr. Joe Dispenza, a neuroscientist exploring the mind's potential to shape reality; and Sadhguru, a Hindu mystic, who deepened my understanding of emotions and thoughts. Yet, it was my religion, Islam, that fuelled my motivation and gave me strength. Through research and reflection, concepts like "sabr" (patience), "shukr" (gratitude), and "tawakkul" (reliance on God) became the foundations for me for build a positive mindset which helped me to shift my mindset from self-pity to self-worth. My mantra in those days was and still is when faced with adversity: This too shall pass.

I have learnt that inspiration can come from various sources when we stay open to reflection and change. Recognizing the profound impact of our words and thoughts on our reality, I consciously chose gratitude, hope, forgiveness, and love as my guiding principles, which I strive to embody to this day. In embracing these guiding principles, I have found a path to inner strength and resilience. They continue to shape my journey, reminding me that even in challenging times, there is always a source of encouragement to be found.

It would be remiss of me not to acknowledge the countless strategies, tools, and practices that anchored my soul and facilitated my healing. Mindfulness became my compass, guiding me to the present moment and allowing me to appreciate life's fleeting beauty and impermanence. Meditation provided a sanctuary, a haven to reconnect with my inner self and find tranquillity amidst life's chaos. Yoga evolved beyond mere physical postures, transforming into a symphony that harmonized my mind, body, and soul. Cognitive Behavioural Therapy (CBT) served as a reflective mirror, highlighting patterns and beliefs, enabling me to rewire detrimental thought processes. Counselling delved into the recesses of my past, bringing to light the roots of my pain and equipping me with the tools for healing. Meanwhile, coaching emerged as my ultimate saviour, directing my focus towards crafting a brighter and purpose-driven future.

But most importantly, discovering my 'ikigai' - a reason for being - proved pivotal. It bestowed upon me the power to embrace my authentic self and the strength to pursue a path that resonated with my true nature. With each day, I evolved into a better version of myself by harnessing the tools I had acquired along the way to elevate not only myself but others as well. This journey has not only fostered my personal growth but has also enabled me to assist others, especially as a coach, in becoming the best versions of themselves.

This narrative is not merely about recounting the challenges faced; infact it is a celebration of the invincible spirit that burns brightly within each of us. Although life frequently confronts us with the inescapable reality of loss and pain, such moments are but fleeting shadows across the vast canvas of our existence. It is our response, our unwavering decision to rise and transcend that truly carves out our character.

Life, in all its complexity, is a tapestry of choices. Every day, I consciously choose the path of gratitude, optimism, and appreciation. In nurturing this mindset, I not only hope but strive to diminish the phantom of despair and anguish that sometimes rears its head within me. Thus with every new sunrise, the shadow of anxiety, loneliness and doubt recedes a little further overpowered by the strength of my Yaqeen.

In life's tapestry, each choice a vibrant hue
I paint with strokes of hope, each day anew

Crafting a life, blissful and serene
Anchored firmly in the strength of my Yaqeen.

Eternal Peace

The sound of falling raindrops
Coming faintly through the window
Eases my troubled soul
The soft caress of the cooling breeze
Blowing gently through the window
Soothes my weary soul
The gradually breaking dawn
Slipping stealthily through the window
Calms my agitated soul
There's euphony
A mesmerising harmony
A strange polyphony
Luring me to sleep
Whispering sweet lullabies
As the raindrops fall lightly near me
The gentle breeze brushes softly over me
The first rays of sun ardently kiss me
I slip finally and
Oh, so blissfully, into
The land of sweet dreams.

~❖~

The Perfect Pearl

You - fragile like glass
Delicate as a rose
Dainty as an eggshell
Fine as bone china
Eons taken to build
Nourish and nurture
Destroyed in a moment
Like a cruelly crushed rose petal
Like a callously handled bone china
Like a carelessly touched eggshell
Scattered, smashed, shattered to smithereens
Once damaged, you are never the same
Broken dreams, aching heart
Lost expectations, unfulfilled desires
Dormant wishes, mislaid faith
Lay waiting patiently
Like a grain of sand
In the heart of an oyster
Expecting to be transformed
Into a perfect pearl.

~ ❖ ~

Metamorphosis

In the cradle of time, I have evolved
Just as a delicate rosebud grows
Into a gorgeous blooming rose
Emitting fragrance gently in the passing breeze.
Just as a small seedling sprouts
Into a strong resilient shoot
Withstanding the harsh winter storms.
Just as a slow crawling caterpillar transforms
Into a beautiful fluttering butterfly
Battling the air currents to stay afloat.
I blossomed, arose and emerged
To embrace life wholly and fully
I now stand in my entire splendour
At the summit of my life
Empowered, emboldened and endowed
It was me
And, only me
That set me free.

~❖~

The Butterfly

I have not changed but evolved
Just as a slow crawling caterpillar transforms
Into a light fluttering butterfly
Allowing the currents to take it
Upwards, onwards and forwards
I blossomed, arose and emerged
From the manacles of
Culture, tradition and society.
As a rose that one day will whither
As a flame that one day will be extinguished
As a butterfly that one day will perish
So, will I one day.
Life is for now
Death is to be.

~❖~

The Rise

How can I fit
In the societal norms
In familial expectations
In friendship groups
In people's lives
That's all I think about.
Like a spinning top
Swirling on everyone's music
But mine
Constantly dancing
On the beat of someone else's drum.
Elated when someone praises me
Deflated when I feel criticised
Up one moment
Down the other
A never-ending pendulum
Of pleasing people.
Exhausted, confused and at times paralysed
A forbidden thought tiptoes in
Where am 'I' amidst this mayhem?
I lay waiting for
A way out
Yearning for an escape
Forlorn, lost, dejected
Death seems like a welcome respite
Yet, a little voice within urges
To release
What doesn't serve me
The weight of expectations
The grip of restless worries
The echoes of past pain
The shadow of self-doubt
To be defiant,
And shout out loud
You are enough
You are perfect
You are YOU.

The Relapse

Today was one of those days
Charged with emotions
Unexplained sadness
Mocking voices
On a loop
I'm alone
Sad and broken
No one to hug me
To hold me
To soothe me
To tell me it's ok
All will be well
We are in this together.
Gusty mists of loneliness
Shrouds the warmth in my heart
With icy hard coldness
Why am I alive
What's my purpose
Will I be lonely always
Niggling thoughts
Immobilising me.
Some days are hard
Harder than others
So easy to relapse
To lose hope
To slip back in darkness.
In the midst of this turmoil
A gentle voice grows stronger
You are not ready
To give up, yet
Just hang in there
There's so much more
To see

To experience, and
To feel.
A wave of gratitude washes over
Helping me to acknowledge
These fleeting moments
These passing feelings
And, the one truth
I may be alone
but I am not lonely.

~ ❖ ~

I Am

I am not my name, my gender or my age
I am not my religion, my caste or my nationality
I am not my job, my family, my skin
So, don't go labelling me
Slotting me in your preconceived boxes
I am more than the sum total of what you see
I am my thoughts, my feelings, my perception
And beyond!
Greater than what you think and believe
More than your narrow presumptions
Preconceived assumptions
I am ME
A unique creation
Not defined by gender, caste or creed
But a mosaic of colours
Beautiful and bold
A medley of songs
Melodious and mellifluous
A deep blue ocean
Magical and mystical
Forceful and fierce.
A complete entity in itself
In complete harmony with the world
Yet, exclusive and exquisite
A shadow, a ripple, a storm
An everlasting imprint
In the moving tides of time.

~ ❖ ~

This is Me

I might be too confident for you
I might be too controlling for you
I might be too aggressive for you
But
I am who I am
I can't change
In fact, I don't want to change.
I need to be accepted on my terms
Who I am
And not who you want me to be
What I am
And not what you want me to be
Accept me or let me go
The choice is yours
Walk beside me or leave me
The decision is yours
I will not fit the mould
You want to cast me in
I am Me
And that's who I'll always be
A complete Being
Embrace me
And, I won't leave you ever
Try to shape me
And, I'm gone forever.

~❖~

Be Still

Many suns have set and risen
Many suns will rise and set
Moments have touched and departed
Moments will touch and depart
Time in its infinity
Tick-toking away
We, in our finiteness
Clamouring away
Chasing dreams, wishes, desires
Like a hamster stuck on a wheel
Running tirelessly but getting nowhere.
Man, in its immense wisdom
Forgets to standstill
To take a deep breath
And, contemplate
A moment is what life is
A moment was what life was
Now, is all we have
And, Now is all we will ever have.
Future uncertain
Past vanished
Present is what is here.
Live day by day
Hour by hour
Moment by moment.
Savouring, what we have
The ultimate gift
LIFE.

~ ❖ ~

One Day

One day when you ask
Will I tell you
What was, and
What could have been
Where we were, and
Where we could have been
One day when you ask
Will I show you
What we had, and
What we could have had
What you gave me, and
What I could have given you
One day, when it's time
Will you understand
The could haves
The would haves
The should haves
Were all ours
And only on that day
Will you realise
What you lost, and
What I gained
On that day, you will not ask
But will only feel
Clutching at your heart
The cold fingers of
Regret.

~❖~

Life

Happy
Sad
Vibrant
Calm
Jubilant
Peaceful
Quiet...
Life!
The tempest
The avenger
The fury
The passion
The madness
The furore.
A circus of emotions
A lover; a friend
A parent; a partner
A worrier; a hopeful
A loner; a companion
A victim; a hero
The colours of life
Playing with you
Teasing you
Invigorating you
Tempting you
Coaxing you
Tantalising you.
Life!
A coy maiden
Inviting
Enticing
Mesmerising
Alluring

Sucking you deeper and deeper
Spiralling
Swerving
Twisting
Ceaselessly, never-ending
Until death
The silent spectator enters
Carnival of life
Falls deadly quiet
Colours vanish
Passion evaporates
Warmth disappears
Just like that
A hush descends.
Life succumbs
Death subjugates.

~ ❖ ~

Legacy

Isn't it enough that we existed?
Why can't we just be
Flowing through time
Freely and untethered
Yet leaving imprints wherever we go
Isn't it enough that we are alive?
In the hearts that we held
In the laughs that we shared
In the words that we exchanged
In the tears that we shed
Isn't it enough that we lived?
To see the sunrise
And the flowers blossom
To imprint a piece of yourself
On those we meet
And, the places we touch.
So then, why do we want
To have our names
Echoed through our children
Engraved in history
Embossed forever in the fabric of life
Why isn't it enough
To simply Be
And then, one day
Not to Be.

~❖~

Alone But Not Lonely

Just as every rose has its thorns
Every bee its sting
Every rise its fall
Every dream its reality
So, does
Happiness carries a halo of sadness.
Life moves
But, under the shadow of death.
Hear the whispers of the moving shadows
As one trudges along life's sunny paths
The silent voices beckoning
As one sails life's peaceful seas
Pay heed to the commotion
Within and, outside
Even in silence
There's an ongoing conversation.
I am alone, but not lonely
In the company of my soul.

~❖~

Kaleidoscope

There's beauty in being alone
Standing still and tall above all
Even when the cruel wind blows
Forcing you to succumb
Or when it whispers sweet lullabies
Lulling you into false hope.
There's colour in the darkness
A rainbow at night
Lighting up every dark cloud
Remain deeply rooted
Yet, sway gently
In the kaleidoscope of time.

~ ❖ ~

A Unique Blend

It's not what I went through that matters
But the fact that I have made it through that counts
All the hardships
All the challenges
All the emptiness
In the core of my being
All the tears
All the pain
All the hurt
In every knock I received
Tells me that life is simply a journey.
Though my path has been treacherous
Tireless in its entity
Strewn with more perils than certainty
Full of heartache
Immense losses
Intense disappointments
Relentless struggle
Yet, it has been a blessing in disguise
Making me who I am today
A unique blend
Of strength and fallibility
Of courage and shyness
Of confidence and self-doubt
Of sweetness and bitterness
Not for anything in this world
Will I change my life
With your life.

~ ❖ ~

The Choice

I choose gratitude, optimism, a forward-leaning stance
Recalling not just storms, but the rainbows' dance
What doesn't serve, I let drift away
Holding the phantom of despair at bay
But above all, I don't merely survive -
I choose, every day, to truly thrive.

~ ❖ ~

The Ending

It is about the stories and not the conclusion
It is about the journey and not the destination
It is about each step and not the journey's end
Love is rare, life is strange
Nothing lasts, and people change
Yet, the journey continues regardless
Taking you through highs and lows
Of pleasure and displeasure
Of fulfilment and unfulfillment
Of satisfaction and dissatisfaction
Of completion and incompletion
You may be lonely in a crowd
But, complete when all alone.
It is not where you are that matters
But who you are that counts.
To be alone
You must understand togetherness
And, to be together
You must understand aloneness.
Life is not just about happy endings
Rather, it's about the stories
Your story
And, mine.

~❖~

My Yaqeen

Life's shadows may often cross our way
Yet pain, in its essence, can't forever stay

Our response, our will to rise and transcend
Carves our path, our story's end.
Life's vast mosaic, choices wide and deep
Each day, gratitude and hope I keep

With optimism as my guiding light
And forward visions, ever bright
I nurture a mindset, so pure and free
Dimming despair's grip on me

With every dawn, a promise clear
Shadows of sorrow will soon disappear

~ ❖ ~

About the Author

Fatima Shaaria Syed, PhD

Fatima grew up in Pakistan and moved to the United Kingdom with her two children in 2004. Fatima has a wealth of experience as an educationist and a change management specialist. She obtained her doctoral degree in Social Policy from the University of Birmingham, UK.

Fatima's personal journey through adversity, particularly her recovery from depression following a traumatic brain injury, has significantly enriched her understanding and view of the world. This transformative period in her life inspired her to establish a coaching business focused on nurturing self-confidence and self-belief in others. Her aim is to empower people to live a more purposeful and fulfilled life.

Beyond her professional endeavors, Fatima finds joy in nature, immersing herself in books, exploring new places, and learning about different cultures and religions.

One of Fatima's most cherished achievements is successfully raising her two children to be resilient, caring and confident individuals.

To Connect:

Email: syedfatimashaaria@gmail.com

Insta:

STITCHEDFROMSORROWS

Printed in Great Britain
by Amazon